Glenn Decides To

D1485279

NO

By
Nina Pitt

Hi, I'm Glenn the ghost.

See my friends over there scaring people!

I want to join them,
but I'm not sure about that.

I hear you ask: "Why?".

Well, it's a little bit complicated.

Every night on my way to my friends,

I get touched by other ghosts!

Some hug me,

some pat me,

some put me
on their shoulders,

and some kiss me.

I hear you wonder:

"So what?".

Well, I just don't like

when someone touches

me, especially

without permission!

It makes me freeze
in my place.

I know, I'm too cute for them to keep
their hands to themselves.

But ghosts are not the same,
some have good intentions,
and some don't.

The worst part
is I can't say..

And the reason is, I think..

I'm too nice, I don't want to be rude.

Mom and dad once said to me:

" Saying "NO" doesn't make you a bad person."

So, I have decided to give it a try.

NO, please don't hug me, I don't like it.

Okay, sorry for that.

It actually worked!

Mom and dad once said to me:
"If "NO" didn't work, then kick and scream".

So, I have decided to give it a try.

NO, please don't kiss me, I don't like it.

I said "NO"!

He didn't listen when I said "NO",

so I kicked him and ran away.

Now, I can say "NO"

and get to play with my friends whenever I want.

NO, please don't carry me, I don't like it.

Okay, sorry for that.

NO, please don't pat me, I don't like it.

Okay, sorry for that.

Hey Glenn, come and..

NO!

I was going to ask you to play with us!

Oh, sorry.

I just got used to saying "NO".

Printed in Great Britain
by Amazon